Internet Activities

for

Criminal Justice
Second Edition

Carolyn Dennis
Criminal Justice Lecturer
Fayetteville State University

Tere Chipman
Criminal Justice Instructor
Fayetteville Technical Community College

THOMSON
WADSWORTH

Australia • Canada • Mexico • Singapore • Spain • United Kingdom • United States

COPYRIGHT © 2003 Wadsworth, a division of Thomson Learning, Inc. Thomson Learning™ is a trademark used herein under license.

ALL RIGHTS RESERVED. No part of this work covered by the copyright hereon, may be reproduced or used in any form or by any means—graphic, electronic, or mechanical, including, but not limited to, photocopying, recording, taping, Web distribution, information networks, or information storage and retrieval systems—without the written permission of the publisher.

Printed in Canada
5 6 7   05 04

0-534-57284-7

For more information about our products,
contact us at:
Thomson Learning Academic Resource Center
1-800-423-0563

For permission to use material from this text,
contact us by:
Phone: **1-800-730-2214**
Fax: **1-800-730-2215**
Web: **www.thomsonrights.com**

Asia
Thomson Learning
5 Shenton Way #01-01
UIC Building
Singapore 068808

Australia
Nelson Thomson Learning
102 Dodds Street
South Street
South Melbourne, Victoria 3205
Australia

Canada
Nelson Thomson Learning
1120 Birchmount Road
Toronto, Ontario M1K 5G4
Canada

Europe/Middle East/South Africa
Thomson Learning
High Holborn House
50/51 Bedford Row
London WC1R 4LR
United Kingdom

Latin America
Thomson Learning
Seneca, 53
Colonia Polanco
11560 Mexico D.F.
Mexico

Spain
Paraninfo Thomson Learning
Calle/Magallanes, 25
28015 Madrid, Spain

TABLE OF CONTENTS

Introduction: Are You Ready to Surf the Internet?	1
Chapter 1: Criminal Justice Today	7
Chapter 2: Measuring and Explaining Crime	11
Chapter 3: Criminal Law	15
Chapter 4: Police: Agents of Law and Order	19
Chapter 5: Policing: Organization and Strategies	23
Chapter 6: Police and the Rule of Law	27
Chapter 7: Challenges to Effective Policing	31
Chapter 8: Criminal Courts	37
Chapter 9: Pretrial Procedures: The Adversary System in Action	41
Chapter 10: The Criminal Trial	45
Chapter 11: Punishment and Sentencing	49
Chapter 12: Probation and Community Corrections	55
Chapter 13: Prisons and Jails	61
Chapter 14: Behind Bars: The Life of an Inmate	67
Chapter 15: The Juvenile Justice System	73
Chapter 16: The Ongoing War Against Illegal Drugs	79
Chapter 17: Cyber Crime	85

INTRODUCTION

ARE YOU READY TO SURF THE INTERNET?

In today's technological world, it is becoming imperative that Criminal Justice scholars be able to utilize a computer and, specifically, maneuver around the Internet. The **Internet** was the result of some visionary thinkers in the early 1960's who saw the great potential in allowing computers to share information on research and development in scientific and military fields.

BRIEF HISTORY OF THE INTERNET

In 1962, J.C.R. Licklider of MIT proposed a global network of computers. As head of the Defense Advanced Research Projects Agency (DARPA), Licklider worked to develop this complex network.

In the meantime, Leonard Kleinrock of MIT and later UCLA developed the theory of packet switching. **Packet switching** formed the basis of Internet connections.

1965 saw the first computer being hooked up with another remote computer over dial-up telephone lines. Lawrence Roberts of MIT connected a Massachusetts computer with a California computer. This exercise demonstrated that wide area **networking** was possible, but that the telephone lines circuit switching was inadequate.

In 1969 the Internet was known as ARPANET and was brought online by the renamed Advanced Research Projects Agency (ARPA). This group initially connected four major computers at universities in the southwestern United States. The four universities were UCLA, Stanford Research Institute, UCSB, and the University of Utah. Each year more agencies were becoming plugged in and today, the world is hooked up or wireless and we are considered an Internet society. The experimental ARPANET was no longer needed by 1990 and was dissolved.

FUN FACT
Who was the first to use the Internet?

Charley Kline from UCLA sent the first packets on ARPANet as he tried to connect to Stanford Research Institute on October 29, 1969. The system crashed as he reached the G in LOGIN!

INTERNET SERVICE PROVIDERS

In 1995, Internet Service Providers (ISPs) such as CompuServe, AOL and Prodigy all started business. The result was an explosion around the world with billions of individuals gaining access to instant global information.

Different ISPs (Internet Service Providers) offer different services. The basic idea behind all of them is to offer data transfer to and from the Internet, and to offer additional services to allow one to access online information. One may also create, implement, and distribute data over the Internet.

> **FUN FACT**
> **Did Al Gore invent the Internet?**
>
> According to a CNN transcript of an interview with Wolf Blitzer, Al Gore said, "During my service in the United States Congress, I took the initiative in creating the Internet." Al Gore was not in Congress in 1969 or in 1974 when the term Internet was first used. Gore was elected to Congress in 1976.

BROWSERS

A web browser is software to facilitate individual computer access to graphical data presented over the Internet on the World Wide Web, or over a local area network in a compatible format. There are a variety of browsers available. The most commonly used are Netscape and Microsoft Explorer.

SEARCH ENGINES

In actuality, a search engine is the software that conducts a search-- regardless of whether or not that search occurs in the context of a big database of web sites, in the context of your web site alone, or even in the context of a database that has nothing to do with the web. Use of the term "search engine" to refer to a tool for searching the Internet has come into play just recently.

Some of the most common search engines include Hotbot, Lycos, Infoseek, Goggle and GoTo.com. If information cannot be located on one search information, switch to another.

CHAT ROOMS

A chat room is an interactive place on the Internet where individuals can chat over the computer. It is much like people talking to people, only better. It is people talking to people that they have never met and online (over the Internet).

There are hundreds of chat rooms available for users. Simply browse around and find one that matches your interests. Chat rooms are a great place for Criminal Justice scholars to get together and discuss current issues in CJ. Be sure and read the section on Netiquette before going to a chat room.

ELECTRONIC MAIL (E-MAIL)

The developers of ARPANET had always considered information and resource sharing as one of their primary goals. As soon as terminals in different rooms could be linked to the same 'host' computer through 'time-share' operating systems, it became possible to leave messages for one another within the same system. Such applications began to appear from 1961 onwards and immediately proved popular among users. However, their limitation was that their use was restricted to the users of a single computer. It was a start, but it was still unbelievably crude.

FUN FACT
The First E-Mail

In 1971 Ray Tomlinson of ARPANET sent the world's first e-mail. The first message was simply addressed to himself, sent from one computer to another, with the text 'Testing 1-2-3'.

Today electronic mail is simply known as e-mail. It is a method of sharing written communications and other computer data over a networked connection.

NETIQUETTE

Netiquette is etiquette for the Internet. In 1986 the rules of accepted behavior over the Internet and E-mail were set out. Here are some of the more common tips of Netiquette:

- Don't SHOUT (by using all capitals).
- If you "must" emphasize, use asterisks (*).
- If you want to show emotion, use an 'emoticon' to laugh :-) or frown:-(, or joke;-)
- Don't spew (repeat your opinion ad nauseam, usually to people who do not want to listen).
- Don't blather (go on, and on and on... a screen, at the most two, should really be the limit).
- And be moderate in your opinions, or you might be guilty of FLAMING.

To flame is to express an immoderate opinion and it can easily lead to flamewars...which degenerate into a slanging-match.

INTERNET ADDRESSES (URL's)

The URL, Uniform Resource Locator, is simply the location of the information over the Internet. Just as we have a street address, information over the Internet has an address.

A URL usually looks like: www.company.com. The WWW stands for World Wide Web and .com identifies a company. Or you may use http://www. and the URL. Most computers do not require this much information anymore.

As you become familiar with the Internet, you will find there is a wealth of information available for the searching. Happy surfing!!

CHAPTER 1

CRIMINAL JUSTICE TODAY

Activity 1-1: National Criminal Justice Reference Service

URL: http://www.ncjrs.org/

Goal: *To learn how to navigate and search the National Criminal Justice Reference Service web site for current literature in Criminal Justice.*

Suppose that you are researching and writing a paper for your criminal justice class. Where would you go to get reliable academic data? A great place to start would be the National Criminal Justice Reference Service.

NCJRS is a federally sponsored information clearinghouse for people around the country and the world involved with research, policy, and practice related to criminal and juvenile justice and drug control.

Let's start with the NCJRS. Go to the web site listed above. Find the button on the left-labeled Corrections. Locate the button entitled Boot Camps. After reviewing the articles, answer the following:

- What are boot camps?
- Where are some of the boot camps located in the United States?
- Who are the primary people being placed in boot camps in the United States?
- What type of punishment are boot camps?

- Are boot camps effective in eliminating repeat offending?

Select the button labeled Courts. Then select the button labeled Capital Punishment. Review the articles in this area and answer the following questions:

- What are the methods of execution in the United States?
- What is the minimum age that the Court has allowed one to be executed?
- How many inmates are on death row in the United States?
- How many female inmates are on death row in the United States?

Next, try the law enforcement button. Click the criminal investigation area. After reviewing the articles, answer the following questions:

- What is an electronic criminal investigation?
- What is the public's attitude towards the use of criminal history information?
- Is eyewitness information valuable to a criminal investigation?
- Is DNA helping to solve more crimes?

Activity 1-2: Gathering Statistical Research

URL: http://www.albany.edu/sourcebook/

Goal: To become familiar with the Source Book of Criminal Justice Statistics and the valuable resources, which it contains.

As a law enforcement officer, a judge or a regular citizen in the United States, you might want to know what crimes are being committed in your area. A great place to get the answers to your questions is the Source Book of Criminal Justice Statistics.

The Source Book of Criminal Justice Statistics is maintained by the State University of New York at Albany and is updated on a continual basis. This is the largest compilation of criminal justices statistics available.

Check out the Source Book of Criminal Justice Statistics web site. Scroll down and find the area labeled Section 1 Characteristics of the Criminal Justice System. Click on Section 1. Scroll down and click on Salaries for police officers and other law enforcement personnel. Read the attached articles and answer the following questions:

- What is the average salary for chief law enforcement officers in the United States?
- What is the maximum salary for law enforcement officers in towns of approximately 10,000 persons?
- What area of the country pays the highest salary for law enforcement officers?
- Where can you make more money: as county or city law enforcement officers?

Go back to the home page of this web site. Scroll down to section 4 Characteristics and distribution of persons arrested. Scroll down and click Arrests in rural counties. Read the attached articles and answer the following:

- What crime was committed most often?
- Who committed more crimes: males or females?
- Which crime was committed the least amount of times?
- Were there more violent offenses or more property offenses committed?
- Which racial or ethnic group committed more crime?
- What is the average age criminal?

CHAPTER 2

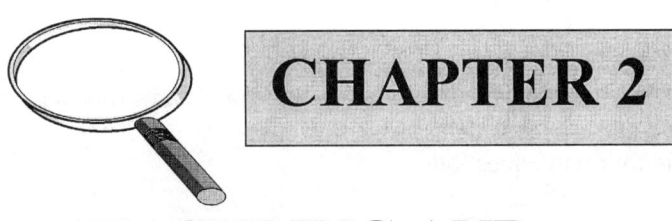

MEASURING AND EXPLAINING CRIME

Activity 2-1: Gathering Crime Statistics

URL: http://www.ojp.usdoj.gov/bjs/

Goal: To use the Bureau of Justice Statistics web site to aid in collecting data and in finding explanations for crime.

Before we can measure crime, we must collect numbers which tell us who is committing the crime, what crimes are being committed and where these crimes are being committed. The Bureau of Justice Statistics collects, analyzes, publishes, and disseminates information on crime, criminal offenders, victims of crime, and the operation of justice systems at all levels of government.

Go to the Bureau of Justice Statistics home page at the URL above. Look under Statistics about the Justice System. Find the word Corrections and click on prisons. This web site will provide statistics regarding prisons in the United States.

- How many inmates are incarcerated in the United States?
- What percentage of these inmates are women?
- What percentage of these inmates is black as compared to the general population of the United States?
- Of those sentenced to prison, what percentage committed a violent offense in 1999?

- Is there an increase from 1990? What is it?

Go back to the home page of the Bureau of Justice Statistics. Look under Statistics about the Justice System. Find Crime and Victims and click on victim characteristics. Review the material and answer the following questions:

- What is the average age of a victim of a violent crime?
- Are Hispanic people more likely to be a victim of a violent crime or are non-Hispanic people more likely to be a victim of a violent crime?
- Which gender is victimized more often?
- Which crimes is gender specific?
- Are married or single people more likely to become victims?

Activity 2-2: Understanding the Causes of Crime

URL: http://www.criminology.fsu.edu/

Goal: To utilize the Florida State University Criminology web site to help in gaining an understanding as to the cause of crime.

As Criminal Justice scholars, one of the topics that we must explore is the cause of crime. Why do people commit crime and why do some people continue to commit more and more crime? These are questions that individuals have been asking for centuries. There are a variety of explanations for the cause of crime and we will attempt to explore some of these explanations.

Go to the Florida State University web site at the above URL. Click on Links and Resources. Scroll down the page and click on Juvenile Delinquency and Juvenile Justice. Scroll down and click on School Crime. Click on the article Violence and Discipline Problems in U.S. Public Schools: 1996-97. Review the article and answer the following questions:

- How often are crimes being committed in our schools?
- Why do these juvenile commit these crimes?
- What are the schools reactions to crime?
- Does the presence of law enforcement officers cut down on the incident of crime in our schools?
- Who is committing crimes in the public schools?

Go back to the home page of Florida State University School of Criminology. Click on the Research button. Scroll down and click on the Juvenile Justice Role Model Program. Go into the Juvenile Justice Role Model Program web site. Review this web site and answer the following questions:

- What are the requirements for the role model program?
- How many hours of community service must be completed?
- Why would you want to become a role model?
- In your personal opinion, is this a good example of methods to eliminate juvenile delinquency?

Activity 2-3: The Uniform Crime Report and Other FBI Files

URL: http://www.fbi.gov/

Goal: To utilize the FBI's web site in interpreting the amounts of crime and to aid in capture of America's criminals.

The statistical analysis, which is thought to be the most reliable, is the Uniform Crime Report. The Uniform Crime Report or UCR is compiled by the FBI and is published on an annual basis. The UCR presents data on crimes, which are known to the police and have been cleared by arrest. Offenses are divided into Part I offenses and Part II offenses. Part I offenses include the following: murder, forcible rape, robbery, aggravated assault, burglary, larceny-theft and motor vehicle theft. There are 21 less serious crimes which compose Part II offenses.

Go to the Federal Bureau of Investigation home page at the URL above. Look to the left. Find library and reference. Under library and reference, click Uniform Crime Report. Find the heading Crime in the United States and click the year 2000. Review the articles and attachments and answer the following questions.

- How many people were arrested in the United States in the year 2000?
- What percentage of these arrests were women?
- What percentage of these arrests is black as compared to the general population of the United States?
- Which crime had the most arrests in the year 2000?
- Which crime had the least arrests in the year 2000?

Go back to the home page of the Federal Bureau of Investigation. Find Most Wanted and click on Most Wanted Terrorists. Review the various descriptions of these most wanted terrorists and answer the following questions:

- What is the average age of the terrorists?
- What is the typical crime that these terrorists have committed against the American people?
- What is the gender of these terrorists?
- Where are most of these terrorists from?

CHAPTER 3

CRIMINAL LAW

Activity 3-1: Current Criminal Justice Legislation

URL: http://www.aclu.org/issues/criminal/hmcj.html

Goal: To be informed of current Criminal Justice Legislation.

As Criminal Justice scholars, it is important that we understand where the criminal law is created and how the process works. The Criminal Law comes from the English Common Law, the US and State Constitutions, Administrative Law and Statutory Law.

Statutory Law comes from the Legislative Branch of Government. Bills are introduced, discussed and voted upon by the members of the State General Assembly or the US Congress. If a bill passes, then it becomes a law.

Go to the American Civil Liberties Union web site at the URL above. Find Criminal Justice in the 107th Congress and click on Take Action.

- Do the ACLU members agree with the death penalty?
- Should eavesdropping be considered legal or illegal if government officials do it?
- Is it constitutional for FBI officials to use undercover software to look into what is happening in Cyber Space?

- What rights does the ACLU feel that disabled Americans should have?
- Do you agree with these publications?

The American Civil Liberties Union has represented many people in court. Go back to the home page of the American Civil Liberties Union. Look under Index of ACLU Criminal Justice Materials. Check out ACLU in the Courts. Review the court cases where the ACLU was helping a defendant.

- What is the typical race of one represented by the ACLU?
- Is the ACLU successful in helping their clients?
- Do you see the ACLU as necessary in the process of fair representation for all people?

Activity 3-2: Researching Case Law

URL: http://www.findlaw.com/

Goal: To be able to locate a Supreme Court Case.

The United States Supreme Court hears approximately 200 cases each year. The decisions in these cases create, change and uphold the law. The United States Supreme Court is considered the Court of Last Resort. When a case is decided at the Supreme Court, there is no other recourse. Their decision is absolute and there is no other place to appeal. Let's check out the US Supreme Court cases.

Go to FindLaw.com at the URL above. Locate Laws: Cases and Codes. Below that find US Supreme Court. Click on that. Browse the 2002 decisions.

- How many cases were decided in the year 2002?
- What are some of the major issues that the Court reviewed at in the year 2002?
- Now look at 2001; 2000.

- Answer the above questions for those years.

Find the case The Amistad, 40 US 518 (1841). Review the case and the decision by the Court.

- What are the facts of the case?
- Does the Court render a fair and impartial decision?
- What is the decision of the Court?
- Is the decision still applicable today?
- Was the decision unanimous?
- Did any Justices disagree with the majority decision?
- Would you have made the same decision?

Activity 3-3: State Constitution

URL: http://www.jus.state.nc.us/

Goal: To examine a State Constitution.

One of the primary sources of the Criminal Law is State and Federal Constitutions. State Supreme Courts use their State Constitution to interpret and compose Case Law like the United States Supreme Court. To properly understand the Criminal Law as it relates to a State Constitution click on the above URL. This is the web site for the Office of Attorney General of North Carolina.

Find Legal Resources and click. Next find NC General Statutes and click there. Look at the top bar and put your mouse over Leg. Information. Now find NC Constitution. Check out Article XI - Punishments, Corrections and Charities.

- What does the North Carolina Constitution say about the death penalty?
- What are the allowable punishments in North Carolina?
- Are charitable organizations allowed in North Carolina?

Now go back and look at Article III the Executive Branch.

- The Executive power of the State of North Carolina is vested in whom?
- What are the qualifications for Governor of North Carolina?
- What are the qualifications for Lt. Governor of North Carolina?
- Who succeeds the Governor of North Carolina if he/she is no longer able to serve?
- What are the duties of the Lt. Governor of North Carolina?

CHAPTER 4

POLICE: AGENTS OF LAW AND ORDER

Activity 4-1: History of Policing

URL: http://www.troopers.state.ny.us/

Goal: To be aware of the history of law enforcement.

Read the message from newly elected Governor George E. Pataki Law Enforcement in the United States was drawn from the model used in Great Britain by Sir Robert Peele. Originally, law enforcement was composed of local volunteers. Today, policing has evolved into a very sophisticated, structured and often technical area of our government. With the invention of automobiles and the computer, American policing has become very specialized.

In this exercise, we want to examine the history of policing. Let's look at the New York State Police Department. Go to the URL above. Explore the home page and click on Introduction. Look to the left of his message and click on History. Read the article entitled Serving the Public Since 1917.

- Who inspired the New York State Police Department?
- When was the New York State Police Department formed?

- Which governing body designated the formation of the New York State Police Department?
- How many men rode out of training camp to begin patrolling the rural areas of New York in 1917?

Now click on the year 1960 to 1970. Read the Article entitled the 1960s. Answer the following questions.

- What was the social climate of the 1960's?
- How many superintendents did the New York State Police Department have in the 1960's?
- What were some of the changes and implementations that occurred within the New York State Police Department?
- What technology the New York State Police Department in the 1960's was using?

Activity 4-2: Law Enforcement Education

URL: http://www.jus.state.nc.us/NCJA/

Goal: To become familiar with law enforcement training.

As policing in American has progressed, law enforcement officers have adopted ongoing training as a part of their professionalism. Many agencies require that an officer be certified at a law enforcement academy before their actual work can commence. After joining a department, officers must continue to be trained, retrained and learn new techniques. With new technology, law enforcement must stay informed as to the operation of that technology and equipment.

Let's examine one of the leading training academies in the United States for local and state law enforcement officers. Go to the North Carolina Justice Academy home page at the URL listed above. Explore this page and click on some of the key buttons. Look at the Mission of the Justice Academy.

- Does this Mission Statement reflect the professional law enforcement officer?
- Does this Mission Statement reflect how we should act as law enforcement officers?
- What is the Mission Statement of the North Carolina Justice Academy?

Go back to the home page of the North Carolina Justice Academy. Look under Training Information and click on Course Descriptions. Scroll down to Traffic and locate the course Traffic Law Update. Review the course description answer the following questions.

- What are the course requirements?
- What is the Course Goal?
- What are the Course Objectives?
- Who is this course designed for or who should attend?

Activity 4-3: Technology and Policing

URL: http://www.iptm.org/

Goal: To examine current technology in the area of law enforcement.

As technology increases for the average citizen in the United States, criminals are taking advantage of the use of technology. Modern police agencies must continue to employ the most current technology to be able to compete with some criminals and to stay ahead of others.

Current technology demands ongoing training and use of available money to purchase these items. Many advances have been made in the use of equipment for investigations, DWI, and an array of other police activities. Let's explore the Institute of Police Technology and Management web site. Go to the web site listed above.

- What types of services do the Institute of Police Technology and Management offer?
- What kind of courses do the Institute of Police Technology and Management offer?
- Will the Institute of Police Technology and Management come to your department and train your personnel?

Look to the right of the home page and click on Computer Courses. Check out the different course being offered in computer technology.

- What types of computer classes are being?
- Are the classes affordable for local law enforcement agencies?
- Is this a good investment of time and money for local law enforcement officers?
- Who is this course designed for or who should attend?

CHAPTER 5

POLICING: ORGANIZATION AND STRATEGIES

Activity 5-1: Becoming a Police Officer

URL: *http://www.lapd.com/*

Goal: To explore the possibility of becoming a law enforcement officer.

Law enforcement agencies throughout the United States constantly have to recruit new personnel. There is a demand by the public for law enforcement to eliminate crime, capture the criminals and serve the community as needed. Law enforcement agencies operate on a 24-hour a day, 7-day a week schedule. There must be personnel on duty at every moment to cover all of the possibilities that could occur within the community

To fully meet the needs of a community, it takes a lot of personnel. Most police departments are constantly looking for new personnel and many are offering a better incentive package for new recruits. As Criminal Justice scholars, many of you might be interested in becoming law enforcement officers. Take a look at the Los Angeles Police Department web site. Go to the URL above. Explore the home page. Look at LAPD Recruitment Brochure and click on Want to Join Us. Check out the various requirements to become an officer with the Los Angeles Police Department.

- Is there a vision requirement? What is it?
- Is there a height requirement?
- What is the average annual salary of a Police Officer I?
- Is there a Pension Plan for Police Officers?
- There are 7 steps to becoming a Los Angeles Police Officer. What are they?
- Would you consider becoming a Los Angeles Police Officer?

Activity 5-2: Criminal Investigation

URL: http://www.belvoir.army.mil/cidc/

Goal: To become familiar with the US Army's Criminal Investigation unit.

Law enforcement agencies have many tasks. Each police department must work on a pro-active and a reactive stance against crime. Throughout the United States area law enforcement agencies are constantly trying to combat crime while having to conduct investigations into crimes that have been committed.

As professionals, most law enforcement agencies have selected certain personnel that specifically conduct only criminal investigations. These employees may have previously been patrol officers that have been promoted to an investigation unit. One of the premiere criminal investigation units is The United States Army Criminal Investigation Command. Check out The United States Army Criminal Investigation Command at the above URL and answer the following questions.

- Where is The United States Army Criminal Investigation Command headquarters located?
- What is the range of criminal investigations conducted by this unit?

- Name 4 technological methods used by this Command to conduct criminal investigations.
- Are there investigations limited to federal property?

Now, look to the left column and click on agent training. Review this area of the web site and answer the following.

- What are the three categories of training for CID personnel?
- What methodology is used in the training of CID personnel?
- What types of communication skills are necessary for a CID Agent?
- Who would be considered support personnel for CID Agents?
- Are CID Agents still deployable soldiers in the US Army?

Activity 5-3: Community Policing

URL: http://www.usdoj.gov/cops/

Goal: To explore Community Policing in the United States.

One of the most recent developments in law enforcement has been the establishment and implementation of community-based policing. Community-based policing is based on the idea that if we have officers in the community interacting with the citizens, the level of crime will decrease. When citizens know their local officers, and have a relationship with them, they are more likely to trust them and to cooperate when needed.

Community-based policing has been established in many law enforcement agencies around the United States. It is proving effective in not only lowering the level of crime in a community, but also lowering the level of fear among the residents.

Let's check out the national community-based policing web site at the above URL. The Community Oriented Policing Services (COPS) Office is an office within the Department of Justice. Find the above URL, go to the home page and answer the following questions.

- What types of money can local law enforcement agencies receive from the Department of Justice to aid in their own community-based policing?
- How does a department apply for this money?

Find Community Policing Resources. Check out Problem-Oriented Policing: Reflections on the First 20 Years. Read the report.

- Who wrote the report?
- What are the fundamental principles of the problem-oriented policing framework?
- How successful has the program?

Return to Community Policing Resources. Look at Promising Practices from the Field.

- What act created the COPS office?
- What is the purpose of the COPS office?
- Which crimes is this office most concerned with?
- What types of technology are most often used in community-based policing?

CHAPTER 6

POLICE AND THE RULE OF LAW

Activity 6-1: The Fourth Amendment: Search and Seizure

URL: http://www.findlaw.com

Goal: To gain an understanding of the Search and Seizure protections afforded to citizens of the United States.

The Fourth Amendment of the United States Constitution states that:

> The right of the people to be secure in their persons, houses, papers, and effects, against unreasonable searches and seizures, shall not be violated, and no Warrants shall issue, but upon probable cause, supported by Oath or affirmation, and particularly describing the place to be searched, and the persons or things to be seized.

As citizens of the United States, we are afforded certain rights and privileges under the law. We must adhere to the law and we can be assured that law enforcement officers are to also operate within the boundaries of the law. This assurance gives us certain guarantees as citizens. Therefore, we can go about our lives and feel comfortable that the government will not violate these rules.

One of the most important guarantees is the right to privacy. The right to privacy can be found in the Fourth Amendment of the U.S. Constitution. This is the amendment where search and seizure procedures are addressed. As a citizen, I am not subject to unnecessary or unwarranted search and seizures of my body or dwelling place.

To explore the Fourth Amendment as it relates to law enforcement, let's look at FindLaw.com at the above URL. Explore the home page. Look at Cases and Codes. Then go to US Federal Laws and click on US Constitution. Scroll down and click on Fourth Amendment-Search and Seizure.

- What is the history of the Fourth Amendment?
- Do the police have to have probable cause to conduct?
- Can the government detain someone without a warrant?
- What is a search incident to arrest?
- Does the Fourth Amendment apply to electronic surveillance?

Activity 6-2: Police Interrogations

URL: http://www.apa.org/monitor/mar00/jn.html

Goal: To understand the rights that a citizen has when the police intend to conduct an interrogation.

In 1966, Ernesto Miranda won his appeal to the United States Supreme Court. Miranda had been found guilty in a lower court of a rape charge. He appealed on the issue that the police should have told him that he could have an attorney present during the interrogation.

Miranda v. Arizona is still considered to be a landmark case in the history of cases heard by the U.S. Supreme Court. In essence, the Court said that law enforcement officers must issue the statement, which has become known as the Miranda warning, prior to a police interrogation. The Miranda warning is as follows:

> "You have the right to remain silent. Anything you say can and will be used against you in a court of law. You have the right to be speak to an attorney, and to have an attorney present during any questioning. If you cannot afford an attorney, one will be provided for you at government expense."

Go to the above web site and read the journal article.

- What did the Court say about the methods used by police in interrogations prior to the Miranda ruling?
- What case did the Court agree to review concerning the voluntariness of a confession?
- Can a confession obtained after the issuing of Miranda rights be considered any more voluntary than a confession obtained before the issuing of Miranda rights?
- What statute did Congress pass two years after the Miranda ruling?
- Did this statute overrule the Miranda ruling?

Activity 6-3: School Resource Officers

URL: http://www.nasro.org/

http://law.freeadvice.com/government_law/education_law/student_locker_search.

Goal: To examine the role of School Resource Officers.

In the era of school violence and troubled youth, it has become commonplace for schools to have a police officer patrol their campuses. This officer is commonly called the School Resource Officer and is assigned this duty on a continual basis.

The School Resource Officer practices a form of community-based policing by interacting with the students, faculty, and administration daily. The idea is that by the officer being involved in the school several objectives will be obtained. First, crime will be lower in the school. Second, the school members will develop a relationship with the school resource officer that will hopefully lead to a relationship of trust and respect.

Having a School Resource Officer in schools raises several issues. Check out the above web site on School Resource Officers and the second web site on the Fourth Amendment and answer the following:

- Can the School Resource Officer search a student's locker without their permission?
- Does the School Resource Officer have the right to search a student's body?
- Does the faculty or administration have the legal right to search a student's locker?
- Does a student have to be present for their locker to be searched?
- Can a student's parents give permission for a locker search in lieu of the student's wishes?

CHAPTER 7

CHALLENGES TO EFFECTIVE POLICING

Activity 7-1: The Use of Deadly Force

URL: http://www.amnesty-usa.org/rightsforall/police/

http://www.kpbs.org/fullfocus/_ep_00_04/

Goal: For the reader to be able to discern whether the use of deadly force by the police is an effective means of social control.

The use of deadly force by police officers has become a hot topic in our country during the last couple of decades. Deadly force is a recurring and divisive issue in communities across the nation.

In <u>Tennessee v. Garner</u>, 471 U.S.1 (1985) the Supreme Court stated that the use of deadly force to prevent the escape of all suspects, whatever the circumstances is unreasonable...It is not better that all suspects die than that they escape. The new rule where a peace officer has probable cause to believe that the suspect poses a threat of serious physical harm, either to the officer or others, it is constitutionally reasonable to prevent escape by using deadly force or if there is probable cause to believe that he has committed a forcible felony involving the infliction or threatened infliction of great bodily harm, deadly force may be used to prevent escape, and if feasible some warning has been given.

Review the above deadly force web sites and answer the following questions.

- Do the police effectively use the power of excessive force to prevent crime in the United States?
- Is the power of excessive being misused or abused in this country?
- What would be considered a reasonable use of deadly force?
- Should there be an organization that polices the police?
- Does race have anything to do with police resorting to the use of deadly force?
- Should we train officers with other options than to resort to deadly force?
- When officers do utilize the use of deadly force, where are they trained to shoot?

Activity 7-2: Domestic Violence

URL: *http://www.ojp.usdoj.gov/bjs*

http://www.police.nashville.org/bureaus/investigative/domestic/default.htm

Goal: To become acquainted with the problem of domestic violence and the challenges that this type of situation brings to a law enforcement officer.

To fully understand the scope of the domestic violence situation in the United States, it is helpful to look at research and statistics that have been gathered by researchers. Locate the Bureau of Justice Statistics web site at the above URL. Find the article "Intimate Partner Violence and Age of Victim, 1993-99". Review this article.

- Do older women have higher incidents of violence or do younger women?

- Which ethnic group is reported to having the highest rate of violence?
- How many women were murdered by their intimate partners during 1999?
- How many men did their intimate partners murder during 1999?
- Who is victimized more often, men or women?
- What was the average marital status of the female victims?
- What was the average household income of incidents of domestic violence against a female?
- What was the average population where a female lived that was a victim of domestic violence?

When law enforcement officers receive a domestic violence call, this is considered to be one of the most dangerous calls for them to take. Domestic violence is considered to be one of the largest problems for law enforcement officers in this country. Review the Nashville Police Department web site concerning domestic violence.

- What is the Nashville Police Departments policy on domestic violence?
- What are the symptoms of abuse or misuse by a partner?
- What is the policy concerning response and follow-up by the responding officer?
- Does this web site provide information to help those in a domestic violence situation?
- What alternatives does one have in a domestic violence situation?
- Should we train officers with other options than to resort to deadly force?
- When officers do utilize the use of deadly force, where are they trained to shoot?

Activity 7-3: School Violence

URL:http://eric-web.tc.columbia.edu/monographs/uds107_index.html

http://www.ussafeschools.org/

Goal: By reviewing the material on school violence and possible prevention methods, we may come to understand some of the challenges facing law enforcement today.

Throughout the last decade we, as a nation, have experienced an alarming increase of violence in our schools. The majority of violence has primarily been in the junior and senior high school age group with fewer incidents at college and primary school levels.

With school violence on the rise on this country, criminal justice scholars have begun to examine the problem more closely. Possible prevention strategies are being examined and implemented nationwide.

This exercise will give you the opportunity to examine some of the recent violent episodes that have occurred in our country. Secondly, it will also give you the chance to check out the preventative measures and programs that are being implemented to eliminate or curb violence in our schools. Examine the above web sites and answer the following questions.

- Do most schools have a plan in place in the event of a school tragedy?
- What are two of the most recent incidents that have occurred in our school in the last six months?
- What are the steps in securing the school during an episode of violence?
- Would School Resource Officers be a preventative measure?
- Does gang activity in our schools predispose violent situations?

- How do we identify gang activity in our schools?
- Do high school students have any expectation of privacy?
- Can we search a high school student's locker without their consent?

CHAPTER 8

COURTS AND THE QUEST FOR JUSTICE

Activity 8-1: The National Juvenile Court Data Archive Web Site

URL: http://ojjdp.ncjrs.org/

http://brendan.ncjfcj.unr.edu/homepage/ncjj/ncjj2/main.htm

Goal: In this exercise the student will be introduced to the Juvenile Court System and gain an understanding of the difference between the Juvenile and Adult Courts.

Juvenile offenders in the United States have a separate court system from adult offenders. The Juvenile Justice system was established in the late 1800's in Cook County, Illinois with the establishment of the first juvenile court. Young people charged with a crime or status offenses are handled differently than adult defendants.

Juvenile offenders must be held in a separate detention area than adult offenders. They are tried in a private courtroom without a jury.

The Office of Juvenile Justice and Delinquency Prevention established the National Juvenile Court Data Archive to provide juvenile justice professionals, policy makers, researchers, and the public with the most detailed information available on juvenile courts.

Review the above webs sites and answer the following questions.

- How do cases flow through the juvenile justice system?
- How many arrests of persons under age 18 were made in 1999?
- What proportion of arrests involved persons under age 18 in 1999?
- How did juvenile arrest rates vary by state in 1999?
- How many murders do juvenile offenders in the United States commit?
- How does juvenile homicide offending vary by age?
- How does juvenile homicide offending vary by sex?
- How does juvenile homicide offending vary by race?
- What proportion of juvenile offenders in custody are being held for violent offenses?
- How does the type of offense resulting in placement vary by race/ethnicity?
- How does the type of offense resulting in placement vary by sex?
- How does the race/ethnicity of juvenile offenders in residential placement vary by offense?

Activity 8-2: Felony Sentences in State Courts, 1998; 1996

URL: http://www.ojp.usdoj.gov/bjs/abstract/fssc98.htm

http://www.ojp.usdoj.gov/bjs/abstract/fsus96.htm

Goal: To become familiar with who and how defendants are sentenced for felonies in state courts.

Each year there are more criminal convictions in the State Courts than in the Federal Courts. Of course, this larger conviction rate would stem from a larger pool of State felony defendants. There are more crimes committed in the State jurisdictions than in the Federal jurisdictions.

Interestingly, the statistics indicate that more felony offenders are sentenced to active prison sentences than receive probation. Statistically, prison sentences are most common, followed by jail sentences, and the lesser percentage of convicted felons are sentenced to probation.

The startling aspect of these statistics is that the majority of these sentenced defendants do not even go to trial. Approximately 94% of guilty pleas accounted for the felony convictions in 1998. This translates into only 6% of those sentenced defendants actually going to trial.

Examine the above web sites. Read the two articles and evaluate the following issues.

- Of those defendants convicted of murder, how many were sentenced to death?
- How many sentenced felons were women?
- What percentage of those sentenced defendants was white? Black? Hispanic or other?
- What was the offense that received the most sentencing?
- What was the average amount of time from arrest to sentencing?
- What was the average prison sentence length given to state defendants?
- Define aggravated assault.
- Define murder and non-negligent manslaughter.
- Define fraud, forgery, and embezzlement.

CHAPTER 9

PRETRIAL PROCEDURES: THE ADVERSARY SYSTEM IN ACTION

Activity 9-1: Indigent Defense Attorneys

URL: http://www.ojp.usdoj.gov/bjs/id.htm

http://www.ojp.usdoj.gov/bjs/abstract/sfids99.htm

Goal: To develop an understanding of how the truly poor receive fair representation for criminal charges which could potentially send them to prison.

Court appointed legal representation for indigent criminal defendants plays a critical role in our nation's criminal justice system. The majority of those charged with serious criminal offenses rely on the service of a court appointed attorney. In 1992, about 80% of defendants charged with felonies used a public defender for legal representation.

States and localities use several methods for delivering indigent defense services to clients. There are public defender programs, assigned counsel programs and contract attorney systems. Review the above indigent attorney web sites and answer the following questions.

- In 1999, how much money was spent to provide indigent criminal defense in the nation's 100 most populous counties?
- How many public defenders are employed in the 100 most populous counties in the United States?
- What is the percentage rate of convictions for defendants represented by public defenders?
- What is the average sentence length for public defender defendants sent to jail or prison?
- What is the racial disparity of those represented by publicly financed counsel?
- Describe the assigned counsel system.
- What is a contract attorney system?

Activity 9-2: Pretrial Release

URL: http://www.napsa.org/docs/faq.htm

http://www.fas.org/irp/ops/ci/whl_release.html

http://www.ojp.usdoj.gov/bjs/abstract/fprd96.h

Goal: To explore the Pretrial Release program in the United States.

After a defendant is charged and arrested, a decision must be made as to their eligibility for pretrial release. If a defendant is found ineligible for pretrial release, then detention in a local jail or detention facility is immediate.

The criteria which the Court or a local Magistrate utilizes to determine whether a defendant is eligible for pretrial detention is based upon several factors: the seriousness of the offense committed; the defendant's criminal history; and the defendant's ties to the community.

If a defendant is deemed appropriate to be released back into the community, pending their court date, then they may be released with or without bond. The Judge or Magistrate may release a defendant with merely a signature or require a posting of money or property to guarantee their return to Court.

Review the above webs sites and discuss the following questions.

- What percentage of federal criminal defendants were ordered to be detained pending their trial?
- Which crime carried a higher percentage of pretrial detention for federal criminal defendants?
- Were alleged first offenders held more often under pretrial detentions than alleged repeat offenders?
- In the case of United States of America v. Wen Ho Lee, why did the Court choose to detain him?
- What were the reasons that Dr. Wen Ho Lee asked to be released from pretrial detention?
- Is pretrial release always free?
- Where can defendants receive assistance in arranging pretrial release?

CHAPTER 10

THE CRIMINAL TRIAL

Activity 10.1: Due Process

URL:
http://www.nara.gov/exhall/charters/billrights/billmain.html

http://www.aclu.org

Goal: The student will become familiar with the basic due process protections offered the criminal defendant under the Bill of Rights.

"No person shall be...deprived of life, liberty, or property, without due process of law."

Imposed on the American Criminal Justice system is a Constitutional requirement for fairness and equity that we term "due process." Due process is guaranteed by the Fifth, Sixth, and Fourteenth Amendments to the Constitution and is intended to protect an individual suspected of criminal activity from the actions of an overzealous government. Due process, in a legal sense, means that legal proceedings against an individual proceed according to the rules and forms established for the protection of private rights. The basic elements of due process include a law that creates and defines the offense, an impartial court with jurisdictional authority over the case, formal and proper accusation, notice and opportunity to defend against the charges, fair trial according to established procedures and discharge from all restraints or obligations if acquitted of the charges.

The web sites listed for this exercise are intended to familiarize you with due process and the Bill of Rights, as well as introduce organizations that challenge the constitutionality of certain legal actions. Visit the above listed web sites and answer the following questions:

- Which Amendment to the Constitution protects against unreasonable search and seizures by the government?
- Which Amendment to the Constitution extended the due process requirement of the Constitution to the states?
- In what city was the Bill of Rights ratified?
- On what date was the Bill of Rights ratified?
- What is the purpose of the American Civil Liberties Union?
- Why do constitutional freedoms often clash with law enforcement?

Activity 10-2: The Speedy Trial Act of 1974

URL:
http://www.usdoj.gov/usao/eousa/foia_reading_room/usam/title9/crm00628.htm

http://www.supremecourtus.gov/

http://www.smh.com.au/news/0005/13/national/national02.html

http://www.wbff45.com/news/legaltip/speedytrial.htm

Goal: Familiarize the student with the Constitutional guarantee of a speedy trial and the difficulties faced by the criminal justice system in meeting the requirements of that guarantee.

According to the Sixth Amendment of the Constitution, "...in all criminal prosecutions, the accused shall enjoy the right to a speedy and public trial." Yet limited judicial and prosecutorial resources, over-burdened court calendars, and the inefficiency of the criminal justice system as a whole often combine to produce lengthy delays in bringing a case to trial.

In Three precedent-setting cases: *Barker v. Wingo* (1972), *Strunk v. U.S.* (1973), and *Klopfer v. North Carolina* (1967), the United States Supreme Court addressed the issue of trial delays. In 1974, the U.S. Congress passed the federal Speedy Trial Act. This act allows for the dismissal of federal criminal charges in cases where the prosecution does not seek an indictment or information within thirty days of an arrest or where a trial does not begin within 70 working days after indictment for those defendants who plead not guilty. The federal Speedy Trial Act applies only to those cases tried in federal court, but *Klopfer* essentially made constitutional guarantees of a speedy trial applicable in state cases.

While few of us can argue with the ideal of a speedy trial for all those accused of criminal conduct, the realities of delivering that Constitutional guarantee are difficult at best. The Federal Speedy Trial Act has been viewed by many in the legal profession as being both short sighted and counter-productive. It has been suggested that the time constraints placed upon the criminal justice system by the Speedy Trial Act have resulted in unnecessary severances, inadequately prepared cases being rushed to trial, and unnecessary dismissal of charges against guilty persons.

- Why was the right to a speedy trial originally included in the U.S. Constitution?
- What pre-trial delays are automatically excluded from the provisions of the act?
- In what year was the federal Speedy Trial Act amended?
- What is the minimum amount of time under the Speedy Trial Act in which a criminal case may be brought to trial?
- What are the most common delays in bringing a criminal case to trial?

Activity 10-3: *Voir Dire*

URL: http://www.crfc.org/americanjury/voir_dire.html

http://www.lectlaw.com/def2/u044.htm

http://www.uscourts.gov/ttb/may96/voir.htm

Goal: The student will develop a better understanding of voir dire and its importance to the jury selection process.

When citizens are called together at a courthouse to form a jury pool, they are questioned by the prosecutor, the defense attorney and by the judge to determine their suitability to serve as a member of the jury. Each prospective juror may be questioned about his or her background, life experiences, and opinions in an effort to determine whether he or she can weigh the evidence fairly and objectively. This process is called *voir dire,* which is an Anglo-French term that means "to speak the truth."

The intent behind the *voir dire* process is to help attorneys uncover biases on the parts of prospective jurors, as well as to identify those individuals who may identify with their case or client. It is a long established legal tradition, and isn't likely to disappear anytime soon. Yet it is far from foolproof, relying only on the potential juror's honesty to weed the qualified from the unqualified.

- How may an attorney use *voir dire* to "challenge for cause?"
- What is a "preemptory challenge?"
- What kind of information do attorneys attempt to uncover during *voir dire*?
- How are potential jurors questioned during *voir dire* proceedings?

CHAPTER 11

PUNISHMENT AND SENTENCING

Activity 11-1: Capitol Punishment

URL:http://www.abcnews.go.com/sections/us/DailyNews/deathpenaltystudy_000612.html

http://www.aclu.org/death-penalty/

http://www.thinkquest.org/library/lib/site_sum_outside.html?tname=23685&url=23685/

http://www.uncp.edu/home/vanderhoof/death.html

Goal: This web exercise will familiarize the student with capitol punishment in America and the arguments for and against it.

Capitol punishment--or the death penalty--has existed in virtually every known civilization and has historically been used to punish a wide variety of offenses. Based on records, it is estimated that around 18,800 legal executions have taken place in America since

1608. Many states and the federal government currently have laws that allow courts to impose sentences of capitol punishment for particularly heinous crimes, most typically crimes involving homicide.

In this exercise you will become familiar with the history of the death penalty, examine problems associated with wrongful convictions and executions, and examine efforts to correct those problems at both the state and federal level.

- In what percentage of cases examined did researchers at Columbia and New York Universities find that a conviction or death sentence was thrown out by a court due to errors or inconclusive evidence?
- Why might a lengthy or detailed appeals process be necessary, or even desirable, in cases involving capitol punishment?
- What percentage of Americans currently support the death penalty?
- What landmark case brought about a moratorium on the death penalty in America?
- When was the Federal Death Penalty Act passed?
- How many offenses carry the death penalty under the Federal Death Penalty Act?
- What are some valid arguments supporting the death penalty?
- What are some valid arguments against the death penalty?

Activity 11-2: Victim's Rights

URL: http://www.ojp.usdoj.gov/bjs/cvict.htm

http://www.thecpac.com/cvrca.html

http://www.ncvc.org/

Goal: The student will gain a better understanding of the increased societal interest in the rights of victims and their families in the criminal justice process.

Prior to the 1970s, the concerns of crime victims were often ignored by the criminal justice system. Criminal justice professionals saw their job as identifying, catching, convicting, and punishing the perpetrators of crimes. The individual victim of that crime was seen – and treated – as little more than a witness.

The criminal law viewed society at large as being the "victim" of the crime, and it was simply the duty of the individual victim to cooperate with the criminal justice system in pursuing justice for society. Even if a victim of crime testified during a criminal trial, the system would often downplay the psychological experience of victimization, including any physical or psychological trauma. The system did little or nothing to ease the psychological or financial burden that the trial process often placed on the victim, nor did it make any particular effort to keep the victim informed as to how the prosecution was proceeding.

Over the past couple of decades there has been a growing national interest in the rights of the victims of crime and their survivors. In 1982, the President's Task Force on Victims of Crime brought national attention to the victim's rights movement and encouraged the widespread expansion of a wide variety of victim assistance programs. In 1996, a victims' rights constitutional amendment was proposed in Congress. Although the bill had wide spread bipartisan support, the bill failed to pass. Despite the failure to pass this constitutional amendment, thirty-two states had passed their own versions of a Victims' Rights Amendment as of the year 2000.

- What is the National Crime Victim's Survey?
- How is the NCVS valuable?
- What was the homicide rate per 100,000 population for the year 1999?
- What is the Crime Victim's Bill of Rights?

- Why did the Victims' Rights Amendment fail in Congress?
- Who is most likely to become a victim of violent crime?

Activity 11-3: Truth In Sentencing

URL: http://www.daily.ou.edu/issues/1999/April-9/truth.html

http://www.washingtonpost.com/wp-dyn/articles/A22403-2002Jan9.html

http://www.heritage.org/library/categories/crimelaw/bg1020.html

http://www.freezerbox.com/archive/2001/06/mcveigh/

http://www.jsonline.com/news/state/jun00/truth19061800.asp

Goal: To introduce the student to the concept of truth in sentencing and its impact on sentencing for convicted offenders.

Truth in sentencing refers to the idea of a close correspondence between the sentence given a convicted offender and the actual time served in prison. Prior to the passage of the Comprehensive Crime Control Act, the difference between the sentence imposed on an offender under the federal, as well as many state, court systems was often significantly longer than the amount of time that offender actually served in prison. Good-time credits and parole often meant that individuals incarcerated for serious crimes spent only a few years behind bars. While this reduction in sentence benefited offenders, it angered victims and the public, particularly when the media would report on some crime committed by an offender who had received an early release.

The Violent Crime Control and Law Enforcement Act of 1994 provided $4 billion in prison construction funds for those states that adopted truth in sentencing laws and could guarantee that serious, violent offenders would serve a set amount of their sentences. By 1999, twenty-seven states had met the requirements for this funding while a significant number of other states were working toward the requirements. Identify some problems for the criminal justice system that might be associated with truth in sentencing.

- When was the Comprehensive Crime Control Act passed?
- Identify some benefits that might be associated with truth in sentencing.
- What percentage of their sentences would violent offenders have to serve in order for states to qualify for federal prison construction funds under the Violent Crime Control and Law Enforcement Act?

CHAPTER 12

PROBATION AND COMMUNITY CORRECTIONS

Activity 12-1: Parole Boards

URL: *http://agencies.state.al.us/pardons/welcome.html*

http://www.usdoj.gov/uspc/

http://www.npb-cnlc.gc.ca/about/about_e.htm

http://www.doc.state.nc.us/parole/

Goal: This exercise is intended to introduce the student to parole boards and their functions in the corrections system.

Parole is a correctional strategy intended to reintroduce incarcerated offenders into society in a gradual manner. It is also intended to promote good behavior on the part of inmates by offering a "reward" of early release. Parole also acts as a way to "free up" much needed bed space in often woefully overcrowded prisons. Yet parole isn't popular among the general public who are often angered that an offender who was "dangerous" enough to be sent to prison in the first place, is now being released before completing his sentence.

Who makes the decision to grant parole to an offender in any given case?

There are two ways in which states may make decisions regarding granting parole to convicted offenders. The majority of states and the federal government have parole boards that determine when an incarcerated offender is ready for conditional release. In many cases these boards also function as parole revocation panels at parole revocation hearings. A parole board's decisions regarding conditional early release of convicted offenders is called discretionary parole. Some states have statutes that result in mandatory parole for convicted offenders, with release dates usually near the end of the inmate's sentence – minus good time credits or other special considerations.

- Should parole boards consider the feelings of crime victims when considering requests for parole? What might be some positive and negative outcomes of this policy?
- What was the result of the Sentencing Reform Act of 1984?
- Who generally serves on parole boards and how do they get the job?
- When was the United States Parole Commission created and why?

Activity 12-2: Shock Incarceration

URL: http://www.doc.state.nc.us/parole/

http://www.youthservices.com/Programs/Facility_Type/Program_Offerings/Victor/Bowie/bowie.html

http://www.state.sc.us/scdc/news/shock.htm

http://www.ussc.gov/1998guid/5f1_7.htm

http://www.drc.state.oh.us/web/reams.htm

Goal: To familiarize students with the concept of "shock incarceration" as an alternative to prison for some youthful offenders.

Shock incarceration programs are intensive, short term, military-style boot camp programs intended to discourage further criminal activity through rigorous activity, education and training, in lieu of a lengthy prison sentence. Inmates sentenced to participate in shock incarceration programs are typically screened to determine that they are both physically and mentally able to withstand the stress of the program. Often convicted offenders must apply for acceptance to the program, and once involved, are bound by a signed contract to participate. The inmate must successfully complete the requirements of the program or he is returned to prison to complete his original sentence.

Shock incarceration programs began to receive widespread publicity in the 1980s and have been touted as an effective, low-cost alternative to imprisonment for non-violent, first time offenders. Yet studies have shown that shock incarceration programs have a negligible impact on recidivism rates.

- Who is typically eligible for participation in a shock incarceration program?
- How does the shock incarceration concept work to "turn around" young offenders?
- Is there a difference in recidivism rates between graduates of shock incarceration programs and those inmates who serve terms in prison?
- When an inmate graduates from a shock incarceration program, what type of supervision is he typically placed under?
- What is the mission of the instructor in a shock incarceration program?

Activity 12-3: House Arrest and Electronic Monitoring

URL: *http://www.kiva.net/~lccomcor/ha.htm*

http://www.jocoks.com/jococourts/cc_jha.htm

http://www.doc.state.ok.us/docs/dochist/Hist1000.htm

http://www.lcaservices.com/pages/services.html

http://www.sharemonitoring.com/

Goal: This exercise will introduce the student to the sentencing alternative of house arrest.

House arrest is a sentencing option imposed by a court that requires offenders to remain confined in their own residences. Under house arrest conditions, offenders may leave their residences only to go to work or school, attend to a medical emergency, or to purchase household essentials. House arrest has been called a viable, low-cost alternative to incarceration for non-violent offenders and those with special needs. Serious offenders placed under house arrest are often required to wear electronic monitoring devices so that probation or parole officers can better monitor their whereabouts. These systems are often highly sophisticated and some use satellite technology to track and locate offenders over a wide geographical area.

Proponents of house arrest argue that it is a socially beneficial alternative to incarceration for many offenders in that it allows the offender to avoid the stigma of imprisonment, while requiring him to pay his debt to society. Critics point out that house arrest may result in the public being exposed to dangerous felons and that it provides little or no punishment.

- How does house arrest benefit the corrections system?
- What type of offender is most likely to be given house arrest?

- How has the privatization of correctional services affected house arrest and other community corrections programs?
- What types of electronic monitoring devices are available?
- How does a year of house arrest compare, cost-wise, with a year of imprisonment?
- What might be some problems with house arrest?

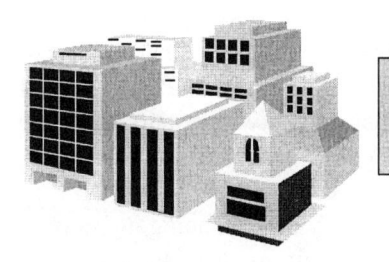

CHAPTER 13

PRISONS AND JAILS

Activity 13-1: Prison Overcrowding

URL: *http://www.qconline.com/progress2000/pjail.shtml*

http://www.geog.utah.edu/~swhite/geog304/wbutler/webpage.html

http://www.ndsn.org/APRIL93/ACLU.html

http://www.ndsn.org/JULY97/PRISON.html

http://www.ojp.usdoj.gov/bjs/prisons.htm

http://www.findarticles.com/cf_0/m1374/6_60/78889717/p1/article.jhtml?term=Supermax+Prison+Florence+Colorado

Goal: This exercise will familiarize the student with the problems and issues surrounding prison overcrowding.

Between 1975 and 2000, the American prison population increased dramatically, and overcrowding became one of the most serious problems facing the criminal justice system. One 1990 study of federal prisons found that they were overcrowded by 73%. State prisons and local jails faced similar, though not quite as serious, overcrowding problems. The management and safety issues brought about by overcrowding, as well as the intervention by the courts in the problem of overcrowding resulted in wide spread new prison construction. This burst of building, as well as judicial intervention, has eased the overcrowding problems somewhat. By 1999, federal prisons were operating at 27% over capacity and state prisons were operating at between 13% and 22% over capacity.

Much of the overcrowding problems facing prisons today was brought about by the incarceration of drug felons convicted under tough federal and state anti-drug legislation. Many of those incarcerated under these laws were young, poor, minority males who could ill afford a good legal defense. Most of these individuals were non-violent.

- What are some reasons that overcrowding has become such a problem for the correctional system? How might these problems be addressed?
- Which states are most in need of new prison space? Are these the states with low or high incarceration rates? Why might states with low incarceration rates be running out of prison space while other states with high incarceration rates have yet to reach full capacity?
- What was the prison population in the U.S. at the end of 1996?
- What impact have tougher drug laws had on prison overcrowding? Why?
- At what capacity were state and federal prisons operating at in 2000?
- What impact have violent offenders had on the increase in the prison population?

Activity 13-2: Supermax Prisons

URL: *http://www.spunk.org/library/prison/sp001611.txt*

http://www.mapinc.org/drugnews/v98.n648.a02.html

http://www.nicic.org/pubs/1999/014937.pdf

http://www-unix.oit.umass.edu/~kastor/cemlarticles/cuinus.html

Goal: This exercise introduces the concept of the Supermax prison and exposes students to advantages and problems associated with this innovative correctional concept.

Prisons in the United States are typically divided into three types: maximum security, medium security, and minimum security. Typically these three prison types can be differentiated according to the relative security risk of the inmates housed in the facility and the level of security maintained by the facility. The Supermax prison is a new concept in confinement intended to house and control the most serious violent offenders.

The United States Penitentiary Administrative Maximum Facility, or ADX, is an ultra-maximum security federal prison located in Florence, Colorado. The ADX holds more than 400 offenders and cost $60 million to build. This facility houses the most dangerous male offenders in the United States, most of whom have sentences of 40 or more years and who will most likely die in prison.

- What type of inmate would be housed in a Supermax facility and why?
- What is the "Alcatraz of the Rockies?"
- What does the average citizen think about the concept of the Supermax prison?
- What was the intent of the Supermax prison, and have they lived up to the expectations of their supporters?
- Identify some human rights issues that might be problematic with Supermax facilities.

Activity 13-3: The History of Prisons

URL: http://www.bop.gov/

http://www.easternstate.com/

http://www.mdgorman.com/prisons.htm

http://www.co.cayuga.ny.us/history/cayugahistory/prison.html

http://www.geocities.com/MotorCity/Downs/3548/facility/newgate.html

http://www.notfrisco.com/prisonhistory/origins/index.html

Goal: This exercise familiarizes students with the historical development of the American prison as a penal institution.

The use of incarceration in prison as a form of punishment is a relatively modern development. During the Middle Ages, it was considered wasteful to confine criminals. Prisons were used to hold political prisoners and those awaiting execution. Corporal punishment was considered an appropriate way to expedite punishment for those convicted of crimes. Because corporal punishment was often very severe, reformers looked for ways to punish those convicted of crimes in a more humane way. Prisons to house and control those convicted of crimes were established in response to concern for the humanitarian treatment of those convicted of crimes. Eventually incarceration became the primary form of sentence, initially for the poor, but eventually for all convicted offenders.

The most important ideas and practices leading to the establishment of prisons were associated with the American Quakers. The Quakers were shocked by the brutal corporal punishments used against convicted felons. Their revulsion with these brutal practices led to the substitution of imprisonment for corporal punishment in those American colonial areas that the Quakers dominated.

- How did the Auburn System develop?

- What was the first modern prison in the United States? Where was it located and when did it open?
- What was the influence of the Quakers on the development of the modern prison?
- Who was Dr. Benjamin Rush?
- What was a "prison hulk?"
- Who was John Howard?
- What was the Pennsylvania System?

CHAPTER 14

LIFE BEHIND BARS

Activity 14-1: Prison Gangs

URL: http://www.dc.state.fl.us/pub/gangs/prison.html

http://www.cjconsultant.com/texgang.htm

http://www.gangsorus.com/gangs/gangprison.html#

http://www.findarticles.com/m1571/n36_v14/21161641/p1/article.jhtml

Goal: This exercise is designed to familiarize students with prison gangs and their impact on the correctional system.

Prison gangs exist in penal institutions all across the United States. In 1996, the Federal Bureau of Prisons noted that prison disturbances increased around 400 percent in the early nineties, indicating that prison gangs were becoming more active. In some states, such as Illinois, almost 60 percent of the prison population belong to gangs. The Department of Corrections in Florida has identified 240 street gangs operating inside the state's prisons.

According to gang investigators, prison gangs are better organized than their street counterparts. Prison gangs evolved within the prison system in California, Texas and Illinois in the 1940s. Unlike street gangs, prison gangs tend to be low-key and discreet. The gang hierarchy monitors members and dictates how individuals behave and treat each other. A serious violation of this gang code of conduct can mean death. Historically, the prison gangs were formed for protection against predatory inmates, but as the gangs evolved and become more organized, racketeering, black markets and racism became factors.

Corrections officials concentrate on inmate behavior in order to identify gang members. Those gang leaders who are identified are not singled out in order to strike "deals" since acknowledging the gang as anything other than a threat to security gives them too much credibility.

The Texas Department of Corrections has reacted most stringently to gangs operating within prison walls. The Texas correctional system has a policy of isolating gang members. Those inmates identified as being part of a gang are placed in a lock down status to discourage membership. This proactive approach to gang control has produced a decrease in violence within Texas prisons. In 1984, 53 inmates were killed in Texas prisons due to gang violence. After the new policy was implemented in 1985, gang related homicides in Texas prisons dropped to five.

- Identify the major prison gangs operating today.
- What similar characteristics are displayed by all of the major prison gangs?
- Where and why did prison gangs originate?
- What Hispanic gangs are operating in Texas prisons?
- Why might prison officials choose to allow gangs to operate?

14-2: Women In Prison

URL: http://womenprisoners.org/

http://www.findarticles.com/cf_dls/m1321/1999_May_1/54488366/p1/article.jhtml

http://www.csc-scc.gc.ca/text/rsrch/reports/r46/toce.shtml

http://www.prisonactivist.org/women/self-defense-not-a-crime.html

http://www.pacifica.org/programs/pnn/prison.html

Goal: In this exercise the student will be introduced to the issues surrounding female inmates in America's prisons.

Over the past few years there has been a dramatic rise in the number of women convicted of crimes and sentenced to terms of incarceration in prison. Today, women are the fastest growing segment of the prison population. It has been argued that this trend is due to things like the change in status of women in the workforce, the greater access to education now available to women and the greater freedoms that women enjoy in our society.

The increase in numbers of women inmates has serious implications for our society. Statistics show that a large percentage of female inmates are single mothers, and that these individuals will continue to be the chief home provider for their children upon exiting incarceration.

Female offenders have different needs from male offenders. This difference stems in part from their disproportionate levels of victimization from sexual or physical abuse, as well as their responsibility for children. Female offenders are more likely to be addicted to drugs and to suffer from some form of mental illness. Many states, in particular those with small female prisoner populations, offer little or no special provision, either in management or programming, for meeting the needs of women.

- Why has the rate of female incarceration increased so dramatically?
- How do the needs of female inmates differ from those of their male counterparts?
- What impact has prior sexual abuse had on the incarceration of women?

- How have issues such as sexual and domestic abuse impacted the incarceration of females?
- What about race? Do African-American women share the same relationship with the criminal justice system as do African-American men?
- Do women receive preferential treatment when it comes to sentencing?

Activity 14-3: Homosexuality and AIDS In Prison

URL http://www.prisons.org/hivin.htm

http://www.igc.org/spr/pdf/122501bill.pdf

http://www.igc.org/spr/

http://prisonactivist.org/pipermail/prisonact-list/2001-December/001433.html

http://prisonactivist.org/pipermail/prisonact-list/2001-August/001086.html

http://www.ojp.usdoj.gov/bjs/pub/ascii/hivpj99.txt

http://www.vix.com/pub/men/abuse/usa-prison.html

Goal: To familiarize the student with the issues surrounding homosexual sex, sexual assault, and AIDS in the prison environment.

In prison argot, the term *wolf* refers to aggressive male inmates who assume the masculine role in a homosexual relationship. A *punk* is a male who is forced into assuming the female role in a prison homosexual relationship – either via sexual assault or extortion. The term *fag* describes naturally homosexual men with effeminate mannerisms. Typically, men described as *wolves* or *punks* identified themselves as heterosexual, and only engaged in homosexual activities in the prison environment. The *fags* generally engaged in homosexual activities prior to entering prison.

While consensual homosexual activity is against prison rules and participants in such relationships are punished by the system when caught, sexual assaults that occur in prison are a serious issue confronting correctional officials. The exact number of prisoners who are sexually assaulted each year is unknown. It is conservatively estimated that around than 290,000 males are sexually assaulted behind bars every year. In comparison, the Bureau of Justice Statistics estimates that 135,000 women are raped each year nationwide.

- Do sexual aggressors in prison consider themselves to be homosexual?
- Why would the Los Angeles County Sheriff's office pass out condoms to gay prisoners?
- What is the primary motive for sexual attack in prison?
- What percentage of male prisoners report having been sexually assaulted while incarcerated?
- Is sexual assault by their peers as much of an issue for female prisoners as it is for males? Why or why not?
- What percentage of male prisoners is HIV positive? What about female prisoners?

CHAPTER 15

THE JUVENILE JUSTICE SYSTEM

15-1: Teenage Suicide

URL:
http://www.intelihealth.com/IH/ihtIH/EMIHC000/20722/8611/192335.html?d=dmtContent

http://www.findarticles.com/cf_dls/m2250/12_38/58531528/p1/article.jhtml

http://www.cnn.com/2002/US/01/08/plane.suicide.mother/index.html

http://www.tott.org/resources.html

http://library.thinkquest.org/12333/page.html

Goal: This exercise is intended to make the student aware of the problem of teenage suicide, the warning signs of suicide and some effective intervention strategies.

Statistics show that suicide is the third leading cause of death among those ages 15 to 25, and it is the sixth leading cause of death among juveniles ages 5 to 14 years. Thirteen of every 100,000 teens took their own lives in 1990, and that number increases each year.

Estimates are that around a half million juveniles attempt to kill themselves each year, and around 5,000 succeed.

Kids face stressors today that were unheard of a generation ago. Things like drugs, peer pressure, parental pressure to succeed, sexual abuse, physical abuse, domestic violence, broken homes, and extreme poverty and hopelessness can lead some young people to believe that suicide is the only viable alternative. Even with the wide variety of stressors facing young people today, some experts believe that kids at risk for suicide can be helped to find other alternatives if their symptoms are recognized in time.

- Identify the warning signs that point toward an individual considering suicide.
- What appear to be some of the factors that have led to such an increase in the numbers of teenage suicides?
- What is the likelihood of someone who has attempted suicide in the past and failed attempting it again?
- How does gender affect teen suicide rates?
- Do people who try to kill themselves always really want to die?

Activity 15-2: Guardian Ad Litem

URL: http://www.guardianadlitem.org/

http://www.rollanet.org/~bennett/bbchild.htm

http://www.govoepp.state.sc.us/children/galhist.htm

http://www.govoepp.state.sc.us/children/training.htm

http://www.casanet.org/library/guardian-ad-litem/gal-e-index.htm

http://www.guardianadlitem.org/training.htm

http://www.lpitr.state.sc.us/bills/3604.htm

Goal: This exercise introduces students to the Guardian Ad Litem program.

When children are involved in legal proceedings or a court case, it is common for everyone involved to be represented by an attorney except for the child. The Guardian Ad Litem (GAL) is a specially trained private citizen, usually not an attorney, who is appointed by the court to represent the child in court and to make recommendations to the court regarding the child's best interests.

Guardians Ad Litem are private citizens who volunteer for this special program and who undergo training to help prepare them for the responsibilities of representing the child. The volunteer Guardian Ad Litem is often the representative for the child before social service agencies and the community, as well as before the court. The volunteer also protects the child during the family crisis and follows the child's progress after the court disposes of the case.

- How did the Guardian Ad Litem program originate?
- Who can be a Guardian Ad Litem?
- What training is required by the GAL program?
- What problems are associated with current GAL programs?
- What are the functions of the GAL in representing the child?

15-3: **Drugs And Alcohol**

URL: http://www.child.net/drugalc.htm

http://www.nida.nih.gov/EconomicCosts/Chapter1.html#1.6

http://www.ctclearinghouse.org/adeter.htm

http://www.whitehousedrugpolicy.gov/publications/drugfact/pulsechk/fall2001/fall2001.pdf http://www.ncjrs.org/pdffiles1/nij/187490.pdf

http://www.narconon.org/html/soln1/SOL4.htm

http://www.npri.org/op_eds/op_ed98/oe090498.html

http://www.druglibrary.org/olsen/dpf/morris01.html

http://www.findarticles.com/cf_0/m2250/n3_v37/20576456/p1/article.jhtml?term=Alcohol+abuse+and+crime

Goal: To familiarize the student with the link between illicit drugs, alcohol, and crime.

A large percentage of young people today have experimented with illicit drugs. Since declining somewhat during the 1980s, drug use by juveniles has been on the increase over the past ten years or so. Juveniles abuse a variety of substances. Studies have shown that 20% of eighth graders have used inhalants and 28% of high school seniors report having engaged in binge drinking. Drug related arrests of juveniles are also on the rise. In 1996, 158,447 juveniles were arrested for drug related crimes. While it is possible that some of the increase in drug related arrests of juveniles may be related to "get-tough" enforcement policies, evidence indicates that more juveniles are utilizing hard drugs than in times past.

Researchers and justice professionals have reported an epidemic of juvenile violence, particularly among teenagers. One recent report noted a significant increase in juvenile arrests, particularly for violent crimes, since the late 1980s. One reasonable explanation for this increase in violent juvenile crime is the rapid growth of crack cocaine markets during the late 1980s.

- How do you determine if someone is chemically dependent?
- What is addiction?
- How much does crime associated with illicit drug and alcohol use cost each year?
- Who is more likely to use drugs – boys or girls?

- How easy is it to get heroin in your locality according to the Office of National Drug Control Policy?
- Has marijuana become more or less popular among teens since 1990?
- What percentage of kids has used alcohol by the end of high school?
- What region of the country has the highest illicit drug use among teens?

CHAPTER 16

THE ONGOING WAR AGAINST ILLEGAL DRUGS

Activity 16-1: Alcohol

URL:
http://www.findarticles.com/cf_0/m0978/4_24/53408424/p1/article.jhtml?term=Alcohol+abuse+and+crime

http://www.findarticles.com/cf_0/m2185/4_12/75249288/p1/article.jhtml?term=Alcohol+abuse+and+crime

http://www.findarticles.com/cf_0/g2603/0001/2603000147/p1/article.jhtml?term=Alcohol+abuse+and+crime

http://www.findarticles.com/cf_0/g2601/0013/2601001313/p1/article.jhtml?term=Alcohol+abuse+and+crime

http://www.findarticles.com/cf_0/m1355/n9_v93/20183558/p1/article.jhtml?term=Alcohol+abuse+and+crime

http://www.1uphealth.com/medical/disease/addiction-substance-abuse-disease/alcohol-abuse-and-alcoholism-94.html

http://www.1uphealth.com/medical/disease/addiction-substance-abuse-disease/alcohol-abuse-and-alcoholism-97.html#7

http://www.aa.org/

Goal: This exercise familiarizes the student with the effects of alcohol abuse and its impact on crime and violence.

Alcohol is quite possibly the oldest known mind altering drug. It is a naturally occurring substance that has been available to, or used by, virtually every known civilization. Along with its long history of use, alcohol also has a long history in which it is associated with violence. Research has repeatedly shown that alcohol use contributes to a wide variety of violent behaviors, and that it is closely associated with such social ills as homelessness, murder, domestic abuse, child abuse and neglect, suicide and other injuries. In the age of the automobile, alcohol use is associated with 50% of all traffic deaths, and ultimately causes about 100,000 deaths in the United States each year, about half of which result from some kind of injury.

Yet alcohol use is legal for the majority of the adult population. Although about 30% of the population does not use alcohol, surveys have shown that more Americans are imbibing today than at any time since WWII. Evidence suggests that around 40 million Americans may be "problem drinkers." Alcohol is big business in the United States, with $104.8 billion in alcoholic beverages sold each year.

- What is alcoholism?
- What serious health effects can result from chronic alcohol abuse?
- What causes alcoholism? Can it be cured?
- What is substance abuse?
- What percentage of prisoners reported being under the influence of drugs or alcohol at the time of their crime?
- How has the correctional system responded to the need for effective drug and alcohol treatment behind bars?

- What is chemical dependence?
- Why does drug and alcohol abuse cause crime?
- What is Alcoholics Anonymous?
- How is alcohol abuse associated with violence?

16-2: Drug Terminology

URL: http://www.nida.nih.gov/DrugsofAbuse.html

http://www.whitehousedrugpolicy.gov/streetterms/

http://www.drugs.indiana.edu/slang/home.html

Goal: Through these sites students will become familiar with the popular idioms used in the street drug culture.

Drugs, whether legal or illicit, may have several names. In fact, some drugs may, when you factor in street slang, have as many as a dozen names. Generally speaking, drugs may be identified according to a brand name, a generic name, a street name, or by how it is categorized as a psychoactive substance.

The name that a manufacturer gives to a chemical substance is the brand name. Brand names are often registered trademarks (Bayer aspirin, for instance). Brand names are used to identify a drug to the public and can't be used by other companies. The chemical name of a drug is that drug's generic name (aspirin or tetrahydrocannabinol). Street names are slang terms used to identify drugs in popular or street culture (weed is a slang term for marijuana). Many of these names originated during the 1960s, though new slang terms to identify drugs on the street are being developed every day. Psychoactive drugs are categorized according to the effects they produce in the human brain. Narcotics slow the central nervous system while stimulants have just the opposite effect.

Drugs, both illicit and legal, are readily available in our society. Yet many people lead lives that keep them well separated from the drug scene – and thus they are unfamiliar with the street terminology associated with the drug trade. As a student, future criminal justice professional, or parent, it can be important to be familiar with the slang used to identify these substances.

- What drug does the term "Sopor" refer to and what are the effects of that drug?
- What drug does the term "Special K" refer to and what are the effects of that drug?
- What is "gaffel?"
- What drug is known as "Animal" on the streets?
- What drug is known as "Boomers" on the streets?
- Identify three hallucinogens.
- Identify the "date rape" drug.

Activity 16-3: The Effects of Drugs

URL: http://www.drugs.indiana.edu/druginfo/

http://www.trashed.co.uk/questions02.html

http://www.brantleycenter.com/fad/designer-microchip.html

http://area51.upsu.plym.ac.uk/~harl/amphets.html

http://www.niaaa.nih.gov/publications/aa27.htm

http://www.addictionscience.net/ASNclass.htm

http://www.freevibe.com/index.shtml

Goal: This activity is designed to make students aware of the variety of effects that psychoactive drugs have on the central nervous system.

All drugs have more than one effect on the body. An example would be how aspirin dulls the pain of a headache, thins the blood, and irritates the lining of the stomach. The drugs that people take for recreational purposes are psychoactive drugs. Psychoactive drugs are those substances that can cross the blood-brain barrier and effect how the central nervous system works. There are 7 major classes of psychoactive drugs. Each of these classes has different effects upon the central nervous system.

Many psychoactive drugs, even some that are seriously abused, have legitimate medical uses. The problems start when people try to use these powerful substances for recreational purposes, usually without understanding what they do, how they do it, and what happens when you mix them with another substance, such as alcohol. Even if you have never used drugs for recreational purposes and have no intentions of ever doing so, it is important to be aware of how these substances work.

- What effect do stimulants have upon the central nervous system?
- How does alcohol affect the central nervous system?
- What classification does marijuana fall under?
- Name three central nervous system depressants.

CHAPTER 17

CYBER CRIME

Activity 17-1: Hackers and Crackers

URL:
http://www.thebestdefense.com/Hacking/index4.html?source=LSM035#Hackers%20Getting%20Caught

http://news.bbc.co.uk/hi/english/world/newsid_1450000/1450463.stm

http://www.infowar.com/hacker/00/hack_012500f_j.shtml

http://www.computeruser.com/newstoday/99/10/08/news11.html

http://it.mycareer.com.au/breaking/20000816/A7373-2000Aug16.html

http://www.cnn.com/2000/TECH/computing/01/21/mitnick.release.01/index.html

http://www.sptimes.com/Hackers/underbelly_of_cyberspace.html

http://tlc.discovery.com/convergence/hackers/hackers.html

Goal: To familiarize students with computer hacking and the problems associated with it.

Goal: To familiarize students with computer hacking and the problems associated with it.

Computers impact almost every aspect of our lives. As a nation, the United States has become dependent upon computers and electronic communications. Millions of American homes and businesses depend upon the security of computer systems to safeguard their personal information as well as to transact business in a secure fashion. Unfortunately, any belief we might have that our computer systems, and thus our information, is secure is misguided.

The term hacker has several different connotations. A hacker might be someone who enjoys exploring the details of programmable systems or a person who uses computers to stretch their capabilities. Hackers may also be described as someone who programs enthusiastically or who is good at programming quickly. A hacker may also be an expert at a particular program, as in 'a Unix hacker.' Unfortunately, the term hacker has gained a negative connotation. In a negative light, a hacker may be seen as a malicious individual who wrongly enters computer systems and attempts to discover, damage or destroy information by poking around where he doesn't belong. According to hackers themselves, the correct term for this type of malicious hacker is "cracker."

The Department of Defense reported 250,000 hacker attacks on military computer systems in 1995. A recently released study by the Computer Security Institute and the FBI's International Crime Squad found that almost seventy-five percent of more than 500 organizations reported a computer security breach within the past 12 months, up from 48 percent a year ago and 22 percent the year before that.

Many hacker attacks go unreported because businesses want to avoid bad publicity. Yet the damage caused by hackers runs in to the billions of dollars annually and can seriously disrupt both private business and government functions. Hacking has become such an issue that the federal government has begun to take the threats presented by hackers very seriously, using terms such as "cyber terrorism" to describe their antics.

- Who was Kevin Mitnick?
- What is a CHIP unit?
- What threat do Russian hackers pose?
- How much did the ILOVEYOU virus cost?
- What does "foo" mean in hacker lingo?
- What is a "back door?"
- Who was John Draper?

Activity 17-2: Cyber Terrorism

URL: http://www.infowar.com/civil_de/civil_c.html-ssi

http://www.pcworld.com/news/article/0,aid,41329,00.asp

http://www.cnn.com/2000/TECH/computing/01/07/clinton.security/

http://www-cse.stanford.edu/classes/cs201/projects/computer-crime/cyber.html

Goal: This exercise familiarizes the student with the concept of cyber-terrorism and its possible impact on society.

Terrorism consists of criminal offenses that are designed to intimidate or coerce a government or citizens in furtherance of political or social objectives. Typically, when we think of terrorism, we think of acts designed to cause destruction and death, such as the Oklahoma City bombing or the September 11th attacks on the World Trade Center and the Pentagon. Yet as awful as these acts are, they directly affect only a limited number of people. Many experts believe that the terrorist of the future will use computer technology to carry out criminal acts that will significantly impact large portions of our society.

Cyber terrorism may be described as hacking into a computer system in order to exploit that system for some serious impact on a society. A terrorist might hack into a computer system that controls electrical power for the entire eastern seaboard, plunging millions of people into darkness and chaos. A hacker might access a computer system controlling air traffic control at a major metropolitan airport, resulting in planes full of people crashing into each other or our communities.

- Why might cyber terrorism pose a greater threat to security and stability than does a terrorist with a bomb?
- How is Bin Laden using telecommunications technology to organize terrorist attacks?
- How much money did the President want to spend to prevent cyber terrorism in 2000?
- Who is William Marlow and what does he do?
- What is the ECTF and what does it do?
- How is the FBI fighting cyber terrorism?

Activity 17-3: Computer Viruses

URL:
http://www.cnn.com/2000/TECH/computing/05/04/iloveyou/index.html

http://www.europe.f-secure.com/v-descs/nakedwif.shtml

http://www.cnn.com/2001/TECH/internet/07/20/computer.viruses/index.html

http://www.bocklabs.wisc.edu/~janda/sladehis.html

http://www.allsands.com/Science/computervirusi_ol_gn.htm

Goal: To familiarize students with computer viruses and how to protect against them.

A computer virus is a self-replicating computer program that interferes with a computer's hardware or operating system. Viruses are typically malicious in nature and are designed to replicate themselves. A virus passes from one system to another, usually via email or shared infected disks. Viruses are also designed to elude detection. Besides viruses there are other harmful computer programs that do not replicate and/or elude detection. These programs fall into three categories: Trojan horses, logic bombs, and worms.

Protecting computers against infection by a virus is not really difficult. Numerous anti- virus software programs are available on the open market that will locate and remove viruses. Anti-virus programs periodically check files for suspicious strands of software code. As with any security issue, prevention is always best. Computer users should download programs only from reliable sites. Users need to know where floppy disks have been before using or sharing them. Finally, beware of junk e-mail, also known as 'spam.' They could contain a virus.

- What did the ILOVEYOU virus do?
- Describe the effects of the NAKEDWIFE virus.
- What is a Trojan Horse and what does it do?
- Who was Fred Cohen?
- Were computer viruses always bad? What were their early uses?